THE BIG MELT

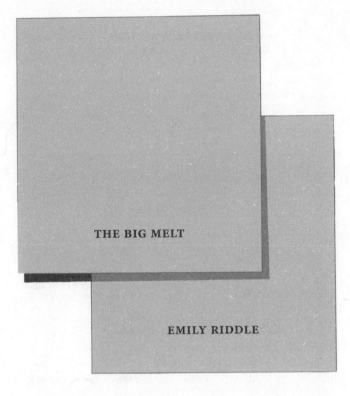

THE BIG MELT

EMILY RIDDLE

NIGHTWOOD EDITIONS

2022

Nightwood Editions
P.O. Box 1779
Gibsons, BC VON 1VO
Canada
www.nightwoodeditions.com

COVER ART: Abbey Riddle
TYPOGRAPHY: Carleton Wilson

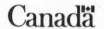

Nightwood Editions acknowledges the support of the Canada Council for the Arts, the Government of Canada, and the Province of British Columbia through the BC Arts Council.

This book has been produced on paper certified by the FSC.

Printed and bound in Canada.

LIBRARY AND ARCHIVES CANADA CATALOGUING IN PUBLICATION

Title: The big melt / Emily Riddle.
Names: Riddle, Emily, author.
Identifiers: Canadiana (print) 20220277745 | Canadiana (ebook) 20220277753 | ISBN 9780889714366 (softcover) | ISBN 9780889714373 (EPUB)
Subjects: LCGFT: Poetry.

Classification: LCC PS8635.I358 B54 2022 | DDC C811/.6—dc23

Contents

THE BIG HORIZON

THE BIG MELT

Tell Me Why

early in our relationship, you tell me the apisci-kahkâkîsak outside your attic bedroom window are annoying. i realize quickly that i am both more careful and cutting with my words. i tell you apisci-kahkâkîsak are bothersome because mostosak left. *left* is a casual word for what happened. apisci-kahkâkîsak have intergenerational trauma because mostosak were brutally murdered. they no longer follow massive herds to eat bugs off their backs in a mutualistic manner. they bemoan this new reality and their squawking is a register of their displeasure. just like me, apisci-kahkâkîsak *awkwardly remain.* i too wake up in the morning and languish. *languish* is a suitable word for what happened. during the second summer of the pandemic, we have been broken up (for the second time) for six months and i am on the road back from the other side of treaty six. as we pass elk island park, nohkôm says, "as long as there are buffalo, there will be cree people. as long as there are cree people, there will be buffalo." i want to believe apisci-kahkâkîsak, mostosak and i will all drink iced tea on a porch together, make light of all that has transpired, talk about the women we have loved.

Audacious

"touch" by little mix is about being a side-chick, which is either a
noble role or a scandal depending on the set-up.

> tbh, i like the idea of a man cooking me dinner and
> not having to wake up next to him, kiss me goodnight,
> see you next weekend. don't keep it all to yourself.

i'm watching some illegal stream of the TLC show *sister wives* and i
wonder if they have considered lesbianism as an option? i mean, one
of these women is definitely queer.

is there anything gayer than never wanting a full-time man?

napew redux

i

i stopped talking to you because you called me pocahontas
even though you stole me a lot of oilers gear, that was still messed up
you sent me a bunch of ANGRY TEXTS IN CAPS LOCK ON MY FIRST-
    EVER CELLPHONE
i laughed in my high school bathroom and pressed delete
i played saxophone in school band and you were a football player
it was never going to work

ii

we sat across from each other at a ramen restaurant in vancouver
it had been six years since i found out over instagram that you got back
    together with (or actually never left?) your white girlfriend
we were trying to be acquaintances, despite having grown apart
    immensely
you told me you do not date indigenous women (anymore) because
    you do not want to interrupt their ascendance to greatness—to
    becoming professors, lawyers, to advocating for our people
you said white women were able to dedicate more time to you and
    that's still true
not sure what frantz fanon would say about that, but he ended up with
    a white girl too

iii

you were my boss, a pitboss at the rez casino and it was the summer
    before i moved away
the thing about being a dealer is men call you a halfbreed cunt and you
    stay up until noon
there isn't much to do in edmonton in the winter at 4 a.m., other than
    eat denny's
once, i showed up to your place in red lingerie and you had fallen
    asleep and didn't answer
in a classic cree move, i sent you a message telling you what you had
    missed
in another classic cree move, you posted a sad public facebook status
    about your fuck-up
when i moved to vancouver, you sent me a care package full of kraft
    dinner

Broken Up

split ends with split ends
open the cupboard and take out the no name coconut oil
pry the fridge door open to check how far gone the eggs are
you have changed from the type of person who throws out food on
    the exact expiry date
to one who inspects it, assumes it's probably okay if not green, runny,
    smelly
i am bisexual and i am not sure i want to do this

mix both and place in hair, trying not to get raw egg all over your face
wrap hair in one of those plastic grocery bags you felt guilty for taking
you have so many tote bags in your front closet awaiting use
sit down and turn on some mindless netflix show
you miss the days of renting a movie and committing to the cause
swipe left on every single polyamorous person on vancouver tinder

some nêhiyawak have truly majestic hair, but majestic is a high bar
    for anyone now
so it's hard not to believe your damaged ends are some sort of moral
    failing
the egg is apparently reducing protein loss
there is debate on whether or not the coconut oil particles are small
    enough to permeate your hair
regardless, this ritual feels productive
go on dates with people who go home and google "plains cree"

rinse out this mask in a cold shower, trying to make sure your hair is not
scrambled eggs and split ends
just split ends and split ends
in the case of hair, you cannot mend what is already broken
chop off your dry ends
and become a new person

Blonde Love

nêhiyaw governance is having an established practice
for when your friend sees their ex at the bar in victoria.

people who were raised on the prairies have a gruffness,
not because of the winters
but rather austerity, discrimination, blue pickup trucks.

this gruffness manifests as
lack of trust,
"don't fuck with my friends,"
initial assumption that you're up to no good.

i don't know how to account
for your non-prairie softness.

underneath it all,
you assume things are going to be okay,
that we can save the world from melting.

i wonder why skydaddy sent me a white girl to love.

i have chosen to move home
and bury myself deep down
in a cocoon of language, ceremony, your thighs.

we leave the bar early to eat mcdonald's in bed,
both with full faces of makeup.
my lipstick first on the mcnuggets
and afterwards on you.

despite the good mess from last night,
you wake up and make your perfectly white bedsheets,
cook a healthy breakfast bowl,
and listen to motown.

i wonder what it is like to be raised in a household
without the legacy of having your babies stolen.
never having a teacher pity you
for your parents not being able to help with math homework,
your dad's credit card in your back pocket.

i trace my finger up your thighs with my acrylic nails
and you shudder because you don't usually date fems.
fem 4 not fem
strands of long dark hair in your blonde world.

Storm Formation

is it sacrilegious to say i was horny for a thunderstorm?
all day we sat on the beach of wâpamon sakahikan
pale halfbreed bodies burning on the beach
foolish not to take the opportunity to slather each other in sunscreen
or admit our true feelings for one another

in june the sky is in transition above nêhiyaw askîy
it's difficult to predict what is going to happen
i can usually tell if it's hot enough for storm formation
but sometimes they roll in unpredictably
like lust for a friend

thunderstorms are just moist heat from the earth's surface rising
positive and negative electrons commune in a cloud
transference happens so quickly that they form lightning
so swift they break the sound barrier
simple enough explanation for a sacred process

after a day of rising heat at the beach
thinking about when 70,000 litres of oil spilled into the lake
and how good your arms looked
i sat in my sweltering third-floor walk-up
as the pressure system outside unleashed

cooling us all down after
being loud and unashamed
lighting up the sky
unleashing tears
resolving imbalance

Next Time When It's −30°C Outside, I Hope You Have Someone With Thick Thighs to Cuddle and They:

- fetch you a glass of water and place it on your nightstand before bed
- listen intently when you tell the same stories again and again, laughing to yourself
- are unfazed when you tell them all the messed-up things about your family
- witness your messy fridge full of good intention, vegetables gone otherwise
- buy you licorice and kiss your forehead every time you get a new poem published
- braid your hair every time an internet troll permeates your prairie bitch exterior
- understand how much you like your own company and hours in the bath
- sympathize with you on days your pessimism takes over
- bask with you on days everything seems possible, marvellous

THE BIG PRAYER

Red

this week in massage therapy, i learned about the importance of the spleen. this week in therapy i learned to ask my friends, "what do you get out of the relationship?" instead of outright saying "DUMP HIM." did you know that if red blood cells are worn out they are ruptured by your spleen and then recycled to make new red blood cells? a very cutthroat process. can you imagine if we applied spleen logic to shitty boyfriends? our system has determined you can no longer be in circulation, but we are willing to work with some of your parts in the creation of something new, refreshed, better.

ORANGE

i remember as a kid telling my dad i must be taking good care of my
ornamental orange tree[1] because it was
F
L
O
W
E
R
I
N
G
and he told me that orange trees reproduce when they're distressed in
order to ensure survival of their kind.

i am not an orange tree

---

1   i asked my parents for an orange tree after seeing that people on television had them
in their backyards. we lived in edmonton, so the best they could do was an ornamental
one that would live in my bedroom. i loved it and my dad and i made orange cakes
with its meagre crop, along with navel oranges from "real" orange trees.

Yellow

very like me to not realize my own loneliness was making me sick. the curse of the eldest daughter to not need anyone. a personality quiz at a corporate job told me i'm an introvert (INTJ) and i believed it. an older man is breaking up with you and says he "wants to be friends," without realizing that is an upgrade from what he is. you realize not everyone is deeply in love with their friends. nêhiyaw elders will tell you that love is about nurturing the growth of an individual. our word for love comes from the word when a plant sprout first emerges from the earth, when it first gains the ability to see the yellow sun above. this is similar to bell hooks' assertion that love is a verb. i want to love you so that you emerge from the earth with a view of the sun, so yellow.

GREEN

if you order a non-alcoholic mojito at happy hour,
people will look at you like you've never known fun.
i've met her a few times.
we went on a few short vacations together,
shacked up for a few months at a time,
but she never moved in her full wardrobe.
alcohol was a boyfriend i had a lot of fun with,
but it did not make sense to see him in my thirties.
it's not because i'm too sacred or whatever,
because drunk aunties are extra sacred.
i am just the ultimate virgo iskwew
who likes to have her wits at all times.

LIGHT BLUE

i think you can fall in love with a colour but
i am stuck in this thought loop
wondering if white people are capable of love
or if this was traded in to facilitate the *big theft*
maybe it's us who lost this ability
tell me you don't have to die a bit inside
to be on either side of this relationship

BLUE

i sew blue ribbons onto pants
and think of maggie nelson,
gatorade, desire vs. yearning
but also about the universe
knowing me as a skybeing
and how to some
the horizon is unnerving
whereas i secretly
hope it devours me
and in this way,
i am the closest to blue

PURPLE

i forgot to buy you a bouquet of flowers,
so i steal you a hanging basket of purple petunias
on the way to your apartment.
for us, purple is the colour of grannies,
so when i want to pray for/to them,
i make an offering in this shade
for all those ohkomimâwak
whose babies were stolen
and those who were stolen from their babies.
the first queen elizabeth liked purple so much,
she banned other people from wearing it.
in defiance of this colour-policing,
i name my daughter mauveine
and teach her that we are a matriarchal people,
that all this land is still ours to care for,
and that her mitochondrial DNA is sassy as hell.
i plant purple petunias in her.

THE BIG KINSHIP

Prairie Fruit

on a flight back from the west coast. i grieve. there are no aerial shots
of the prairies. prior to them being cut up. like oranges for a kids'
soccer game. my dad tells me. the only fresh fruit available in edmon-
ton in his childhood. were oranges, apples and bananas. i am a prai-
rie fruit. saskatoons, strawberries, blueberries. when nêhiyaw babies
have their firsts. we feast on blueberries. to celebrate them. to protect
them. to be delicious. if we do this again. perhaps the prairies will
liberate themselves. prairie fruit will reign again. rain again.

Louise

i have loved you since i first heard your name on a field trip to fort edmonton park. these tours are so catered to white students, they assume no one in the audience is your relative, despite your wealth of descendants. affluence = the number of cousins you have. you knew this, i am sure, though you lived in one of the most impressive houses this city has ever seen.[1] within our kinship system, you are really my grandmother since i am descended from your sister. a matrilineal reminder. nohkôm nitanskotapan × 2. your ancestry.ca profile on my family tree says that you were born in 1783 in the beaver hills and died in 1849 in the same place. how strange i have gotten to know you this way. there are no photos of you, and i have not found any descriptions, beyond that you had brown skin. you are the daughter of a nameless cree woman and an unknown father. some people say your maiden name was belly, others say your name was shining star. you are most famous for bagging john rowand, who became the chief factor of fort edmonton thirteen years after you saved him following a horse accident. this is the story i loved as a child—you saved this white man, not the other way around. this is before we were unsure about saving white people. when they say you were "wed in the laws of the country," they mean you were wed by indigenous law, which means the white guy you married entered a web of kinship (obligation) and you could leave if you wanted (you were not property). he married you even though you were a decade older and already had seven children. what power! some people romanticize unions of the fur trade, but let no one erase your diplomacy, nohkôm nitanskotapan. there is proof that your husband considered leaving you for a white woman (this is wholly common to this day). but he stayed

---

1   it was reportedly the first house west of wînipêk that contained glass windows.

with you until you passed. after this, he left your territory. he decided to flee the kinship web.[2] it was as if he knew he did not belong here without you.[3]

2   later white people would attempt to remove us from our kinship webs instead of entering them. this is partially why i know you through the internet.

3   however, he died downstream in fort pitt of a heart attack on his way to montreal. he didn't make it out of our territories alive. his bones were exhumed months after being buried due to a pre-mortem request to be buried in montreal. he was known to be a large, hated man and some say his fat was made into soap at fort pitt. notably, one of the white men i dated moved to europe years after we broke up.

Learning to Count

peyak:
the hotel cecil, where our kokums used to drink, is now where the
    white-collars buy $17 salads
you are now one of these white-collars
the place we used to sun dance is now home to million-dollar
condos
you can't afford a one-million-dollar condo

niso:
ndns make the best hockey fans but we usually can't afford tickets
ndns make the best catholics but jesus never came for us
and you told me that's because we didn't need him
i never smiled so big as when you told me that

nisto:
women told to wear long skirts
stay home
be quiet
be sneaky

newo:
asinîy
pahpamiyhaw asinîy
wants to return home

nîyânan:
two men
Métis
nêhiyaw
drove all afternoon
from misâskwatôminihk to amiskwaciwâskahikan
speeding past askîy cut into neat squares
asked to pick up firewood on their trip, they stopped in a gas station
they laughed to themselves
what would the ancestors think of plastic-wrapped firewood?
but mosôm mostos became paskwâw mostos
and now the world is covered in plastic

nikotwâsik:
ripped canada flag on top of the band office
the worst coffee imaginable
the cousins who are always in the band office
oh coffee mate, thou are so grossly delicious

têpakohp:
who's your mom?
hmmm.
who's her mom?
oh, yes.
sad look.
eyes meet.
conversation changes

ayênânêw:
i stood by your asinîy kehkwahaskanihk ohci
except it wasn't a gravestone at all
i don't know why none of the aunties got them
peeling wood crosses it is then
a cousin told my mom he took them all out to mow the lawn
"looked in the little brown bottle," he said
and forgot where they went
so now all these peeling wooden crosses are all mixed up
nêhiyawak didn't bury people: we suspended them in trees
but can you imagine?
oh, but the bruno sisters love roses

kîkâmitâtaht:
advice: you have to be careful of that sâkihitowask
because when an elder tells you how to pray for your ideal person
they might arrive at a less than ideal time
sâkihitowin isn't cheap
but it won't cost you any sôniyâw either

mitâtaht:
êkîkiyâmêwisiyit
but they're not anymore

mitâtaht peyakosâp:
treaty day
shake hands
shiny $5 bill
redcoats
big list/big binder
who's a capital *I* Indian
whose relatives married too many white guys
and got booted out of treaty (status)
the sun's shining
rivers still flow, even if they're dirty as heck
grass appears to be growin'
since i'm still mowing it

nîsosâp:
don't take shit from anyone
eat them for breakfast
and dessert
laugh
and cry
maybe too much

nîstosâp:
bombs under the powwow grounds
no one listened to the elders
don't sled there
you'll get blown up
every time an ndn builds a golf course
creator giggles at us

nêwosâp:
she left us
from the heights of a bridge that joined two cities
desperately looking for her
we called out her name into the river
her love playing love songs
already knew she was gone

niyânanosâp:
a father buries his son near the sun dance grounds
boy goes home, to the stars
father prays to be the one buried beside him

nikotwâsosâp:
homeland swagger
bougie ndns drinking eight-dollar beers on a patio
gwich'in, Métis, nêhiyaw, 'nish grannies don't approve
once a nehiyaw granny told me that if she saw me in the city in pants,
she'd rip them off me
women should wear skirts
saw her in sobeys with jeans on
i was wearing a miniskirt

têpakohposâp:
wîsakeyitamostamatâw
close your eyes
âhkwan
do you see lights?
lights jumping around means spirits are visiting you
no, my girl, don't be afraid
your ancestors protect you from bad spirits
even the colonizer ones?
wisakahwaw
yup, even they love you
…but the nêhiyaw ones need you to stick around more

Belongings

sometimes i think about my settler ancestors:

the scottish/swedish/danish/irish ones

who hauled their bodies over the ocean

to eventually become dirt

to become ndn land itself

to eventually become me

a nêhiyaw iskwew

we are in the end just material

these ancestors came over on ships made of trees from their lands

i doubt anyone asked these trees what they thought of this

or if they wanted to leave

knowledge keepers here say that trees communicate

from coast to coast through their roots

do you think some european trees miss their relatives?

or know they are over here?

do they feel sad they don't belong like i do?

have they learned to live together with the original trees?

How to Overthrow Canada via Infographic

prince philip died
and i wish i could celebrate
but my teachings don't allow me
to find joy in the death of an old man
the treaty six confederacy sends condolences to the queen
on the passing of her husband
as one should do
when your mother's husband dies
i eat a pint of ice cream
with the acknowledgement
that i will never live to be ninety-nine
due to factors beyond my control
the queen seems immortal
while my ndn friend group faces tragedies
despite experiencing an ongoing genocide
we have a healthier relationship to death
the queen sends my chief a pastel pantsuit that matches one of hers
he is supposed to receive a new outfit every three years as per our treaty
inside the package, a letter reads
i'm sorry
i can't
don't hate me[1]

---

1   real ones will understand this reference.

Bruno Blues

Donna
Loved
Singing
Big Hair
Had Sisters
And Babies
Didn't Live
Long Enough
To Meet Me
I Visit Her
Every Day
In the Mirror

Wildest Dreams

do you ever see "i am my ancestors' wildest dreams" posts on facebook?
and think to yourself,
i am the coworker who microwaves salmon
and then eats it in her cubicle
i have been known to wear the same pair of socks,
for three days in a row.
run away from that good love,
when someone readily wants to give it.
"it has been three days since you received this email,

                                                            would you like to respond?"
buy new underwear,
just so i do not have to do laundry.
swipe right on white boys on tinder holding fish,
shirtless on top of a mountain.
run away from conflict,
even though love means a good fight sometimes.
"it has been five days since you received this email

                                                            would you like to respond?"
avoid looking at my bank balance,
to add up my total oat milk latte expenditure.
periodically get acrylic nails,
so as to not chew mine down to the quick.
the ndn ancestors i imagine love each other without restraint,
gifted to them by WASP ancestors and disassociated urban life.
"it has been a week since you received this email,

                                                            would you like to respond?"

Maskwa Ponders Revolution

what if instead of looking all humble during the settler national
anthems, ethan bear sat on the ice with his legs crossed?

i sat in the arena wishing for peaceful refusal.
thinking about how the syllabics on his jersey are alive,
wondering what they think of this timeline.

i purposely stay seated and stuff popcorn into my face and people look
at me with confusion while o canada *is belted out.*

i read a lot of marx in my early twenties
and remember thinking i'd have to stop watching NHL
if was going to be a real ndn communist,
but i didn't.

sometimes i wonder if maybe hockey is quelling a proletariat
revolution on the prairies?

perhaps the 2006 hockey riots in edmonton
served as a dress rehearsal
for when the post-oil class wars begin.

fanon says violence is a cleansing force but a commitment to non-
violence is a core nêhiyaw belief. i sit with both of these thoughts often.

for prairie ndns,
the results of the 1885 resistance lives within us all,
a wound that refused to heal, forever ones who bit the hand who
gave us mouldy rations.

we have this reputation now of being overly peaceful, of ignoring
the efficacy of direct action.

i think about the children from the battleford industrial school who
were forced to watch
as eight kin were hanged for organizing against the queen.
a warning not to resist the new world order.

the crown has been organizing against us ever since, despite
committing
to become kin.

sitting in the back seat of a truck on the way through battleford,
i think about how mistahi maskwa lived peaceful refusal,
what he would have thought of the hockey and the bears who came
after him.

Dinosaur Economics

Ask the dinosaurs. What happened to them? We asked one of our elders, "Why did those dinosaurs disappear?" He thought about it for a while and he said, "Maybe they didn't do their ceremonies."

—Leroy Little Bear

i wanted bitumen to be made of dead dinosaurs. why did i want these ancient kin to be passively implicated in the fossil fuel industry? it felt like an appropriate way to romanticize the disaster of the tar sands. how tragic to be killed by a meteorite and for your remains to warm the planet into disaster millions of years later. perhaps this is a means of climate change coping. a weird one. however, in my research for this poem i concluded that the ford f-150s of alberta are not burning dinosaurs to propel themselves. in fact, petroleum, natural gas, etc. come from plankton, marine organisms and bacteria from oceans three billion years ago. so the entire term *fossil fuels* is a strange, incorrect one. others were also attached to dinosaurs as part of the energy sector but for different reasons. the term *tar sands* still remains jarring to me as someone who grew up in alberta. maybe this surprises you about me, but the programming in this province began early. i distinctly remember learning about "have-not" provinces in elementary school, how "we" paid for their free daycare. what i did not learn was that none of the land below the depth of a plow was surrendered in treaty, that my nêhiyaw ancestors would have never understood children going hungry in a land of such prosperity. there was prosperity here before money, oil wells and pipelines; there will be prosperity after those cease to be here. in 2006, my working-class family of four (three out of four of which are treaty indians) received a cheque for $1600 from the klein government due to the surplus of a booming oil economy. that year we went on vacation, packed up a station wagon to the brim, fuelled by old sea creatures.

Worms

the first thing you do when you get off the phone
open the cree dictionary app
maybe the ancestors stuck in this app have some answers
sounding out syllables
hoping for some comfort
the nêhiyawêwin word for cancer provides a visual of worms, maggots
these worms multiply and devour your insides
cancer is simply an undesirable growing too quickly
cells that have decided to do their own thing
the day you find out about your mom
you can barely say what the news is to him
he takes you on a walk up to a lookout in stanley park
and it seems unappreciative to be sad with a view of the ocean
he takes you out to dinner at a noodle restaurant
they are out of noodles
you go back to his apartment and fool around
he leaves your bra on
you appreciate this quiet gesture of kindness
because suddenly your breasts are a liability
after this, you walk around
until your plastic birkenstocks blister your feet
and you sob tears in public about everything
but it rains enough there that no one can tell
or no one cares, because it's vancouver

Panties and Pillowcases

that summer had eight terminal points
an octothorpe of endings
every day i woke up with a mouthful of vinegar
spit it out onto freshly laundered sheets
took them down to the basement laundry room
old men picking through my bin of panties and pillowcases
while i was in queue for the dryer
nothing is ever dry on the salish coast
maybe only a discount paperback
found on a sale table out front of a used bookstore
cover fading in the fleeting sunshine
think of the author of this threadbare poetry collection
perhaps a peristeronic boyfriend that no one liked
an older millennial who still used eggplant emojis
that boyfriend and i both with incurable lethargy
trying to muscle through clouds
parting the condensation with such fervour
i didn't order this brain cocktail
nor did i ask to be part of this bootlegging operation called canada
the border of a turtle's carapace has twenty-eight sections
thirteen pentagons inside
i have twenty-eight days between each full moon
thirteen full moons
to pray for/request clean sheets
unbridled sunshine
an end to the bootlegging operation

It Flows Here, But

i

i call my parents a few times a week on facetime
we hang out and watch CNN and they fight over whose turn it is
to carry me around
while they do dishes
and i remember the most important intimacies are never spectacular

ii

part of why i wanted to move home, beyond escaping an abusive work situation, was to renew my relationships to the moon, to the river here, to my mom who had recently finished cancer treatment. i lived away when she did chemo, radiation, fasted. i remember as a child thinking how it seemed impossible that i came from this person and that i would most likely live on the earth without her at some point. that still seems impossible to me. when i returned to treaty six, i actively asked for help in learning more about my family's history on this land and i received this help. i grew up in the city and always knew i was from here but since we were removed from this place in favour of settlement, we often don't talk about the city as territory. it is very counter to vancouver where the three host nations actively assert their sovereignty over the land that became urban. what does it mean to be an uninvited guest?

iii

ask the moon for forgiveness
on the way to the corner store
buy a slurpee and a chocolate bar
a blue ring emerges
every time you stare at her fullness intently
she doesn't mind that you stare at her craters,
her cellulite, if you will
ask the moon to
take away all my sickness and defects
how to explain?
we are both pitiful
and deserving of love bubbling over

iv

one of the ways my mom ensured we had a relationship to the land in the city was through creating art together. sometimes she would let my sister and i skip school and the three of us would go down to the river to sketch the contours of the banks, the lines of sediment, the clouds above us. it was never explicitly communicated as a way to connect to place, but she taught us to sit and observe where we are by example. i never doubted that i was an artist because my mom showed my sister and i all the ways in which we could be. to make beautiful things, and mistakes, and to experiment are core component of being nêhiyaw, as i understand it. one of the great rewards of being an artist is the possibility of new supplies. on these days when we skipped school, we were each given our own sketchbooks and a box of charcoal. new art supplies seemed like a luxury and i think they always will. only later did i learn about the spiritual significance of charcoal, of the protection of scorched earth.

V

other days when we skipped school, we would go to the world water-park, in west edmonton mall (WEM), which my dad helped construct when he was a plumber. both waterways (the river and the wave pool) are integral to how the city conceptualizes itself. the world waterpark is home to the largest indoor wave pool in the world and the "edmonton river valley" is the "largest urban parkway in north america." knowing both these facts is just proof that edmontonians will forever be insecure with to what degree their settlement is *admirable, successful, permanent.*

vi

if you take your teachings seriously
you'll come to the realization that the wave pool in WEM
is extra sacred
mistahi nîpîy
all that water in one place
it's even called blue thunder
which sounds like the ndn name of some guy you'd fall in love with
in a seminar

years ago, i went on a river valley walk with dr. dwayne donald, who is a papaschase cree band descendant. donald has taken many people on these indigenous history walks, but it wasn't until i lived in vancouver and was home for christmas that i learned the story about the fort edmonton gardens told by donald through conor mcnally's film *ôtênaw*. conor showed me a first cut of the film in his basement after we ate a bowl of homemade ramen. donald talks about how each rendition of fort edmonton had a garden and how these gardens were regularly raided by ndns, who did not yet have a solid understanding of private property. thousands of beaver pelts were exported from our territories and carrot "theft" was offensive. donald shared that eventually a fence was built around the garden, but the ndns persisted in helping themselves to the gardens, turning the fence into a bonfire. later in the 1870s, the decade when treaty six was made and we began moving onto reserves, the fort employed an armed guard to protect the garden. now, many things have armed guards, if you think about it, such as a hockey arena not far from the final location of the fort. i tend to tomatoes in a community plot named after the man who removed the papaschase cree.

not far from this hockey arena is ninety-seventh street, which is contentious territory as we see the gentrification of the neighbourhood and the forced erosion of chinatown. ninety-seventh street was named namayo avenue by a settler from prince edward island who had learned nêhiyawêwin on his travels in manitoba. namew is the name we have for the dinosaurs (sturgeon) who reside on the bottom of the river. they have seen a lot of shit, you could say. despite a white man giving the street his name, i have heard it was because ndns would fish for sturgeon in the north saskatchewan river and sell them to chinese people along ninety-seventh street. this is a beautiful story (one i wish was true!) but the first chinese person documented as settling in edmonton was chung (john) kee who arrived in 1890. he set up a laundry not far from frank oliver's *edmonton bulletin* headquarters, the very paper that advocated for immigration policies banning chinese folks. in 1912, when edmonton and strathcona were amalgamated we lost these names in the favour of a numbered grid. there are of course a few exceptions, like wayne gretzky drive, named after a man who would certainly advocate for an armed guard for the garden.

ix

people think prairie ndns didn't garden
but we accepted potatoes as the new buffalo
even though we didn't want to
and then weren't allowed to sell that new buffalo
when we were too good at growing them
our stories tell us that buffalo will re-emerge from the earth
if we lovingly remake the earth for them
remove the armed guard
ask the moon for help
hug your mom

Icy Futures

rivers like when you know their real names, it's only polite
 the northern pike laugh when you say saskatchewan
 but appreciate the effort
 of the girls living on the banks.
as kids, our parents drove my sister and i up to the columbia icefield,
 told us to fill a water bottle straight from the source,
 showed us the signposts of the receding hairline of ice
i can't bring myself to visit now, to face the glacial m

e

l

t

i

n

g

in the treaty negotiations, we told them this agreement was to last
 as long as the rivers flow
 that the mountains were too sacred to be included in this treaty
 as was the water (obviously)
 we have been warned!
that glaciers that feed the arteries of our territory will vanish one day,
 and then what will happen?
i used to panic about this particular treaty clause
 i still panic thinking about our river no longer flowing
 i was full of despair the summer the TMX pipeline was quietly
 doubled underneath it,
while another plague hits the people,
 who live along one of the rowdiest parts of the river
there was a small comfort to be savoured when i was told...
 the *rivers flowing* references the fluid of nêhiyawak who give birth
 (not just women)

this is one of the ways in which i am connected to treaty in perpetuity,
    a demonstration of diplomacy, aqueous intentions, fluid continuity
today, the ndn sisters who drink glacial water surrounded by tourists
with their mom,
        (who would cut a bitch if anyone tried to steal them, as she was)
    are just as much the *flow,* as the droplets from the mountains

Holy Beings

on the day the chief of kâ-awâsis announces they have confirmed 751
bodies in unmarked graves outside the residential "school" in their
community, i google things like:

when will the sun run out of fuel?

at what point will we run out of drinkable water?

is a nation without a language spiritually stateless?

next week, jason kenney is fully "post-pandemic" reopening the prov-
ince for july 1, so i call a bakery and ask them to write "êkîsâkihitakok"
on a fifty-dollar cake and book myself a massage covered by my city
health benefits.

   the matriarchal line of my family tree reads like: prairie bourgeois,
  smallpox, residential school, day school, child welfare, middle class

i wear an orange shirt to work as some kind of balm to my being,

       but i've sat in the sun enough this summer,
    that i get sympathetic looks from settlers that walk by me
     they are bombarded by the reality they maintain

consider this:

    i can see right through your entire bodily facade and i know
   the difference between white guilt and you pitying me
      for being a prairie ndn

i am so blessed to be born who i am and
i want every urban nêhiyaw baby to feel that too, to know that they are

        holy beings

            walking on land full of prayers for their well-being
and it is not their fault they

                        don't know that

THE BIG HORIZON

Please Write a Poetry Book in Syllabics[1]

i want to complicate the term *sacred*, she told me
to make holy
sacerdotal: priestly
sākris: to make a treaty
studying words allows you to
see the desecration
of connection
what people
gave up
to be white
"but i don't want to live in this alphabet anymore"
we have a much better one.

---

[1]   i commit to writing one of these before i die.

nikâwiy and i watch youtube documentaries

as i grew up, i became friends with more people who had nêhiyaw moms but were not raised with them for various reasons. mine is all fire sign and saskatoon pie. i never take for granted that i have her, that she roasts me every day, and that we still cuddle while watching TV in her bed.

nikâwiy and i learn ᒣᑭᐯᑊᐃᑲᓇᐸ

my mom and i go to nêhiyawêwin class twice a week and the good
woman brings me homemade soup for dinner. i am a cree brat.

nikâwiy and i refuse to acknowledge the settler state

the mood: it is july 1 and my mom picks me up in her vibe station wagon with miley's "wrecking ball" blasting, an apt song for a day celebrating occupation. she is wearing an orange dress. we have pre-ordered our iced coffees and BLTs. the afternoon and much else is ours to claim, together.

Indigiqueer Archives

the people who wrote the *indian act* weren't thinking about millennial ndn gays bringing babies into the climate apocalypse. they presumed we would all die or assimilate, not sundance or question gender essentialism. how strange that i'm attached to the idea of my hypothetical babies being *indians*,[1] but will raise them with the freedom to grow into their own gender. there is currently no way to remove yourself from the indian register, though you can opt to be added if you are eligible. while some provinces allow people to register their babies with their gender as x, you must either be male or female in the indian registry.[2] i'm comforted and tickled that while i read about my ancestors in census documents, fur trade journals, treaty payment lists and scrip records that all note that we are either m or f, our descendants will come to know us through our twitter feeds, selfies and poems.

---

1   under the current *indian act*, this requires that i reproduce with someone else who is recognized as an *indian* since I am registered as 6(2). to me, it is very illuminating to put this act in conversation with queer familial ethics of parenting with more than two partners or raising children that aren't biologically yours. archaic legislation has haunted my dating life since before i even had a dating life.

2   this was true at the date this poem was first written but changed in 2021. now you have the ability to register with an x gender marker.

kikway itwe "joy"

i wish this book was just about cree joy but there are so many things ob-
fuscating that timeline, so i write it as much as i can, even if it's fantasy

on the way to a BBQ on a house just off commercial drive, i ask what
kind of burgers you want me to bring and you remind me you can't eat
bison because it's your clan

the delicate balance of cree joy requires: CBD gummies, govern-
ment-sponsored therapy, metamucil, probiotics, osteopathy, praise

on the way to the golf course built on stolen enoch cree nation land,
we blast billy talent and talk about how we could never live without
the vastness of the homelands again

the delicate balance of cree joy requires: regular ndn mario kart
nights, eight glasses of water a day, a week without microaggressions

on the way to mcdonald's in your jeep, we talk about disappointing
white lovers, how we ultimately believe so deeply in our ability to ro-
mantically flourish

the delicate balance of cree joy requires: dr. pepper slurpees, REM
sleep, a bowl of vegetables, lactaid, a night out dancing

on the way to our regular park spot where we drink iced oat milk
lattes, i pick you up and we both remark on each other's new outfits
and new beadwork

the delicate balance of cree joy requires: pep talks from your dad, new
poetry books, no disciplinary obligation to be joyful

Cree Girl Explodes the Political Project Called "Alberta"

After Billy-Ray Belcourt's "Cree Girl Explodes the Necropolis of Ottawa"

i stared at the sandstone dome of the alberta legislature so long that it started to disintegrate. it seemed to be doing that on its own, how this "temple of democracy" was covered in tarps during maintenance. but this time the sedimentary grandfathers squished into this symbol of occupation were fully revolting. the beavers were alerted from their metropolis to the west and filed in to dismantle the wooden furniture and fixtures. they spared the kwagiulth totem pole on the grounds and called upon horse relatives to carry it back to the west coast. the nearby magpies giggled to themselves, feasting on the snacks of over-paid political staffers. once the building had returned to the earth, the last iteration of louise's fort edmonton mansion emerged from the lawn-bowling green. she wrote emails from the dead to each of her descendants. none of us questioned this because our ancestors had powers beyond emails. we had learned that the only way to survive climate upheaval was to accept the nonlinearity of time and realms. we had not figured out how to communicate across those borders but opening ourselves to it was half the battle. all of louise's descendants who were single moms moved into her house and built other houses on the grounds of the non-existent alberta legislature. there was no chief factor. there was no premier. there were only okihcitâwiskwêwak and those who understood their authority.

Revitalize Me

i live in "downtown edmonton." this means i'm part of the "revital-
ization of the downtown core." it's possible to gentrify on your own
land. i often get mail that says stuff like "dear neighbour, please read
the following update about the rossdale power plant development."
this power plant, which has been decommissioned, was built on top
of a traditional burial ground in 1902, one that contains my relatives'
remains. 1902 is twenty-six years after this land became treaty six
territory, three years before alberta became a province, twenty-eight
years before the *natural resource transfer act*. this place is called a bur-
ial ground rather than a cemetery because the word *cemetery* has legal
implications which would make it more difficult to build a gondola,
or some granville island–esque market, or some other bullshit. a pri-
vate company is doing historical tours of the plant. i commented on
their FB page "do people whose ancestors are buried under this plant
get free tours?" they respond with "what a great idea, send us a DM."
the power plant was fuelled by coal mined from the banks of the river.
maybe i am just recovering from too much western political theory,
but there is probably a lot to be said about the transformation of coal
into energy that displaced one sovereign power for another. i am sure
that the administrative assistant who puts these notice envelopes in
the mail is unaware that they are sending FYI notices about the dese-
cration of the recipients' family graves, which is a particularly sharp
act of violence. *i would define violence as a transgression of natural law.*
i would define whiteness as the annihilation of natural law from one's
collective being. sometimes being nêhiyaw means only being able to
feel one hurt at a time, in order to preserve one's bodily integrity as a
four-bodied being. so when i receive these envelopes, i go visit these
ancestors, read them the new propaganda that came in the mail, and
we laugh knowing our love is permanent.

Notes

Previous versions of some of these poems appeared in a chapbook entitled *Ancestors and Exes,* published by Glass House Press, which was graciously edited by Jason Purcell, Matthew Stepanic and Matthew James Weigel.

"Tell Me Why" and "Prairie Fruit" were published in *The Fiddlehead* (No. 290, Winter 2022).

"napew redux" appeared in *Prism International* 57.3 (2019).

"Broken Up" was published in *Funicular Magazine* 2.1 (2020).

"Blonde Love," "Please Write a Poetry Book in Syllabics" and "Indigiqueer Archives" were published in *Contemporary Verse 2* 43.3 (2020).

"Storm Formation" was published online by *Plenitude Magazine* in November 2020.

"Louise" appeared in *PRISM International* 59.1 (2020). This poem is about a relative who is thought to be buried at Dead Cop Park near my home in Edmonton. I thought about her a lot during a pandemic. She helped me write this book.

"Learning to Count" was shortlisted for the 2020 CBC Poetry Prize and published on their website.

"Belongings" was published in *This Magazine* (Summer 2020).

The brilliant and funny Leroy Littlebear quote at the beginning of "Dinosaur Economics" comes from his public presentation at the Ipperwash Inquiry held in Forest, Ontario on October 14, 2004.

"It Flows Here, But" was published online under the title "sohkeciwan maka" as part of the Ociciwan Contemporary Art Centre's inaugural show called amiskwaciwâskahikan and was published on their website.

"Icy Futures" was published in *Room Magazine* 45.2 (2022).

"nikâwiy and i watch youtube documentaries," "nikâwiy and i learn ᒪᐦᐲᐧᐃᐧᐃᐠᐅᐊᐧ," "nikâwiy and i refuse to acknowledge the settler state" and "Revitalize Me" were published in MAMANAW PEKISKWEWINA AMISKWACIWASKAHIKAN: GIFTS OF ART which was care(rated) by Cheyenne Rain LeGrande.

"kikway itwe 'joy'" was published in *Riddle Fence* 43 (2022).

"Cree Girl Explodes the Political Project Called 'Alberta'" appeared in *Room Magazine* 43.4 (2020).

Acknowledgements

Thank you to my mom and sister for teaching me about being an artist and a nêhiyaw iskwew. My dad has always been my backup, source of advice on everything, encouragement through all my bullshit and the bullshit of the world.

This book was started in Denendeh, conceptualized in S̱kwx̱wú-7mesh, səl̓ílwətaʔɬ" and xʷməθkʷəy̓əm territories, and completed on my own ancestral lands. All these territories held me in different ways, at different times in my life. Ayi hay to the caretakers of these territories and may they be returned to the rightful stewards. I am so lucky to be part of a legacy of nêhiyaw artists creating on our territories, imagining a future of us, here, forever.

Both Joshua Whitehead and Brandi Bird made this book so much better with their careful edits. I am truly so lucky to write in an era where I get to work with editors who approach my work with such care and rigour. All the editors of poems in this book made them so much better, and me a better writer.

I exist in an ecosystem of Indigenous brilliance! All these folks are changing the world: Matt, Jess, jaye, Billy-Ray, Brandi, Brooks, Meghan, Evan, Justin, Conor, Jas, Jessie, Nickita, Jordan, Cheyenne, Autumn, Sam, Selina, Molly, Hunter.

Thank you to my extended Edmonton crew which makes it such a cool place to live and create, including Michelle, Matthew, Jason, Madeline, Rose-Eva, Eric, Batul.

Ayi hay to nôkhom Jo-Ann Saddleback for teaching me about colours, matriarchy and so many other things.

Richard Van Camp for helping me with "Learning to Count" and encouraging me to publish poetry even though that seemed so far from a possibility! You were right.

This book was supported by funding from the Canada Council for the Arts and the Edmonton Arts Council. Get paid to write your poems.

Grateful to you for reading and witnessing.

PHOTO CREDIT: MADISON KERR

About the Author

Emily Riddle is nêhiyaw and a member of the Alexander First Nation in Treaty Six territory. A writer, editor, policy analyst, language learner and visual artist, she lives in amiskwaciwâskahikan. She is the senior advisor of Indigenous relations at the Edmonton Public Library. Her writing has been published in the *Washington Post*, the *Globe and Mail*, *Teen Vogue*, *The Malahat Review* and *Room Magazine*, among others. In 2021 she was awarded the Edmonton Artists' Trust Award. Emily Riddle is a semi-dedicated Oilers fan and a dedicated Treaty Six descendant who believes deeply in the brilliance of the Prairies and their people.